URANUS
The Sideways-Spinning Planet

by Ellen Lawrence

Consultants:

Suzy Gazlay, MA
Recipient, Presidential Award for Excellence in Science Teaching

Kevin Yates
Fellow of the Royal Astronomical Society

Published in 2014 by Ruby Tuesday Books Ltd.

Editor: Mark J. Sachner
Designer: Emma Randall

Photo Credits:
NASA: Cover, 6, 8, 10, 11 (top), 12, 13 (top), 14–15, 16, 18–19, 20–21; Ruby Tuesday Books: 7, 9, 22; Science Photo Library: 17; Shutterstock: 11 (bottom), 13 (bottom); Superstock: 4–5.

Library of Congress Control Number: 2013939987

ISBN 978-1-909673-16-8

Printed and published in the United States of America

For further information including rights and permissions requests, please contact our Customer Service Department at 877-337-8577.

Contents

Words shown in **bold** in the text are explained in the glossary.

Welcome to Uranus

Imagine flying to a world that is hundreds of millions of miles from Earth.

As your spacecraft gets near, you see a beautiful, blue ball in the darkness of space.

You fly much closer and dive into swirling **gases** and clouds.

You will find nowhere solid to land, though, on this faraway world.

That's because the huge, blue ball is made only of icy gases and liquids.

Welcome to the **planet** Uranus!

No humans have ever visited Uranus, but a spacecraft has. In 1986, *Voyager 2* became the first and only space **probe** to fly past Uranus.

This picture was created on a computer. It shows how it might look to fly very close to Uranus.

The Solar System

Uranus is moving through space at over 15,000 miles per hour (24,000 km/h).

It is moving in a huge circle around the Sun.

Uranus is one of eight planets circling the Sun.

The planets are called Mercury, Venus, our home planet Earth, Mars, Jupiter, Saturn, Uranus, and Neptune.

Icy **comets** and large rocks, called **asteroids**, are also moving around the Sun.

Together, the Sun, the planets, and other space objects are called the **solar system**.

Most of the asteroids in the solar system are in a ring called the asteroid belt.

An asteroid

The Solar System
Uranus is the seventh planet from the Sun.

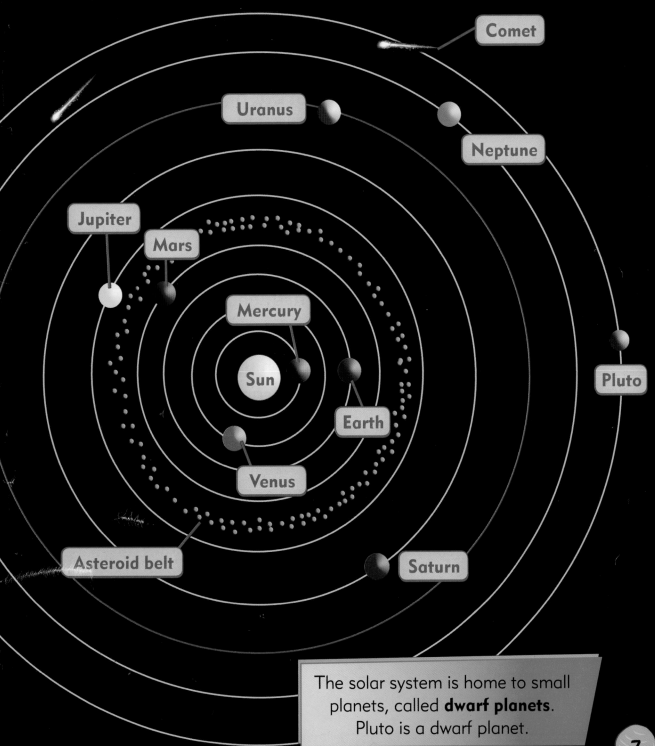

Comet

Uranus

Neptune

Jupiter

Mars

Mercury

Sun

Earth

Venus

Pluto

Asteroid belt

Saturn

The solar system is home to small planets, called **dwarf planets**.
Pluto is a dwarf planet.

Uranus's Amazing Journey

The time it takes a planet to **orbit**, or circle, the Sun once is called its year.

Earth takes just over 365 days to orbit the Sun, so a year on Earth lasts 365 days.

Uranus is farther from the Sun than Earth, so it must make a much longer journey.

It takes Uranus just over 84 Earth years to orbit the Sun.

Can you imagine waiting 84 Earth years to celebrate your first birthday in Uranus years?

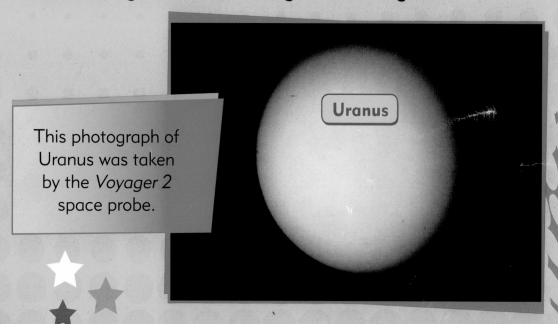

Uranus

This photograph of Uranus was taken by the *Voyager 2* space probe.

To orbit the Sun once, Earth makes a journey of about 584 million miles (940 million km). Uranus must make a journey of about 11 billion miles (18 billion km).

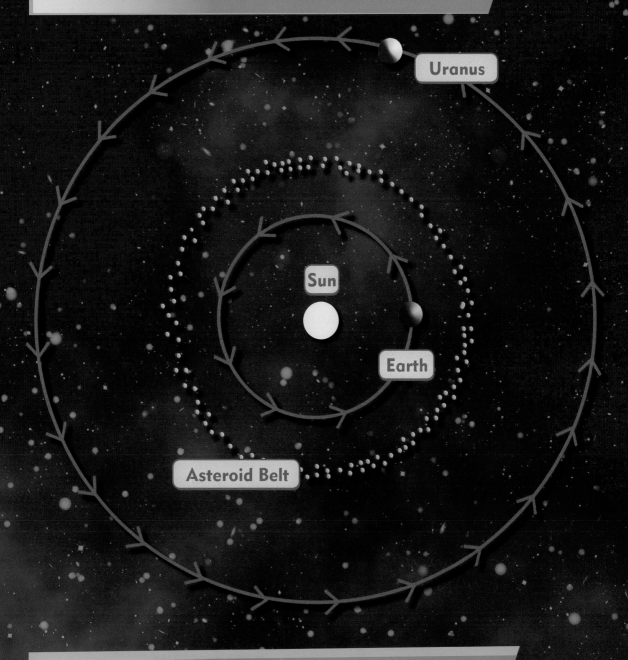

Uranus

Sun

Earth

Asteroid Belt

In this picture, we've taken away all the planets in the solar system except for Earth and Uranus. Now it's easy to see Uranus's super-long journey around the Sun!

A Closer Look at Uranus

Uranus is the third-largest planet in the solar system, behind Jupiter and Saturn.

Unlike Earth, which is a rocky planet, Uranus doesn't have a solid surface.

The planet has an outer layer of gases and clouds called an **atmosphere**.

Inside the atmosphere, winds blow at up to 560 miles per hour (900 km/h).

Beneath its atmosphere, Uranus is a huge ball of icy liquids.

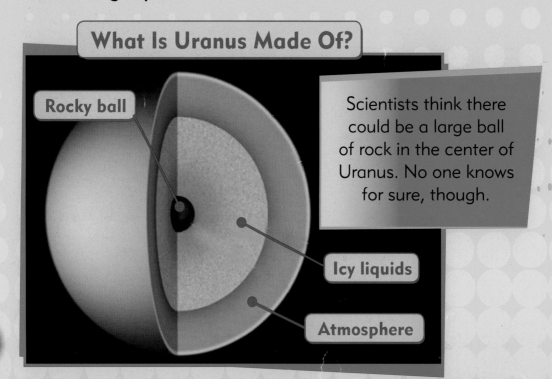

What Is Uranus Made Of?

Rocky ball

Scientists think there could be a large ball of rock in the center of Uranus. No one knows for sure, though.

Icy liquids

Atmosphere

Earth

Uranus

Uranus is nearly four times wider
than our home planet, Earth.

How Uranus Spins

As a planet orbits the Sun, it also spins, or **rotates**, like a top.

As they rotate, most planets are in a nearly upright position.

Uranus, however, spins on its side!

Some scientists think that Uranus once rotated in an upright position.

Then, it was hit by another huge space object.

This **collision** knocked Uranus onto its side, and turned it into a sideways-spinning planet!

Jupiter

This picture shows the planet Jupiter. Jupiter rotates in an upright position.

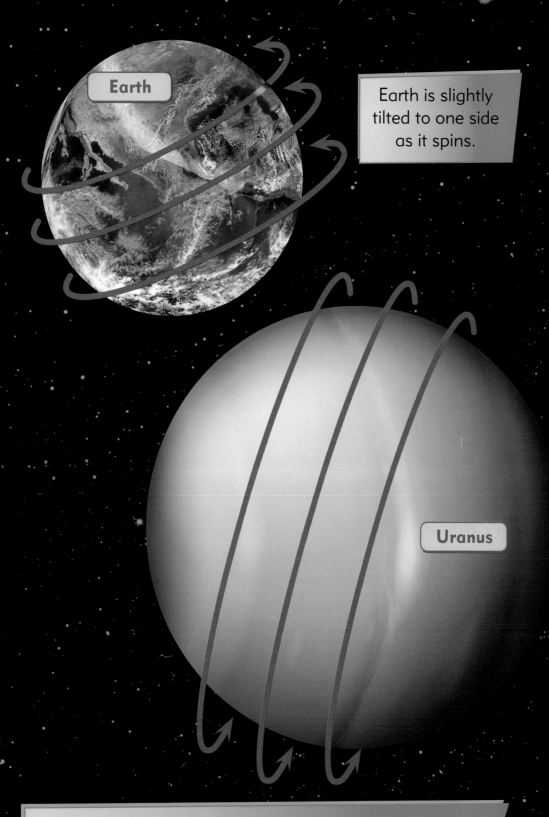

Earth

Earth is slightly tilted to one side as it spins.

Uranus

Uranus spins on its side. It also spins in the opposite direction than most other planets. You can see this by looking at the arrows around Uranus, Earth, and Jupiter.

A Family of Moons

Uranus has a large family of small worlds orbiting around it.

These icy, rocky space objects are the planet's **moons**.

Earth, our home planet, has just one moon.

Uranus has at least 27 moons, and scientists think there may be more!

Many of Uranus's smallest moons are only about 10 miles (16 km) wide.

That's tiny compared to huge Uranus, which is about 31,000 miles (50,000 km) wide!

Ariel

This close-up picture shows the surface of a moon named Ariel (AIR-ee-uhl).

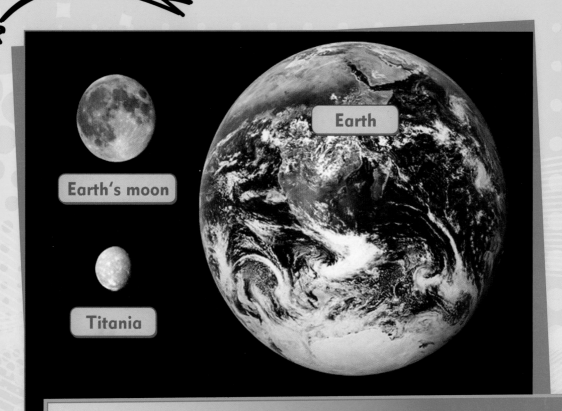

Earth

Earth's moon

Titania

Uranus's largest moon is named Titania (ty-TANE-ee-yuh).
It is nearly 1,000 miles (1,600 km) wide. That's about
half the size of Earth's moon.

Miranda

Uranus's moon
Miranda has giant
canyons on its surface.
The canyons are 12
times as deep as the
Grand Canyon!

A Surprising Discovery

In 1977, scientists watching Uranus through powerful telescopes saw something surprising.

They discovered that there are rings circling the planet.

No one had ever seen the rings before.

Other telescopes and the *Voyager 2* probe have helped us learn more about the rings.

We now know that there are at least 13 faint rings circling Uranus.

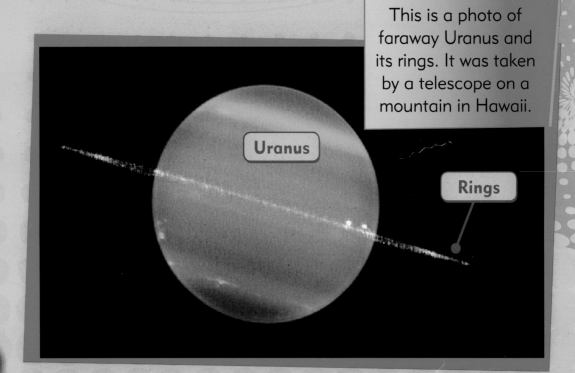

This is a photo of faraway Uranus and its rings. It was taken by a telescope on a mountain in Hawaii.

Uranus

Rings

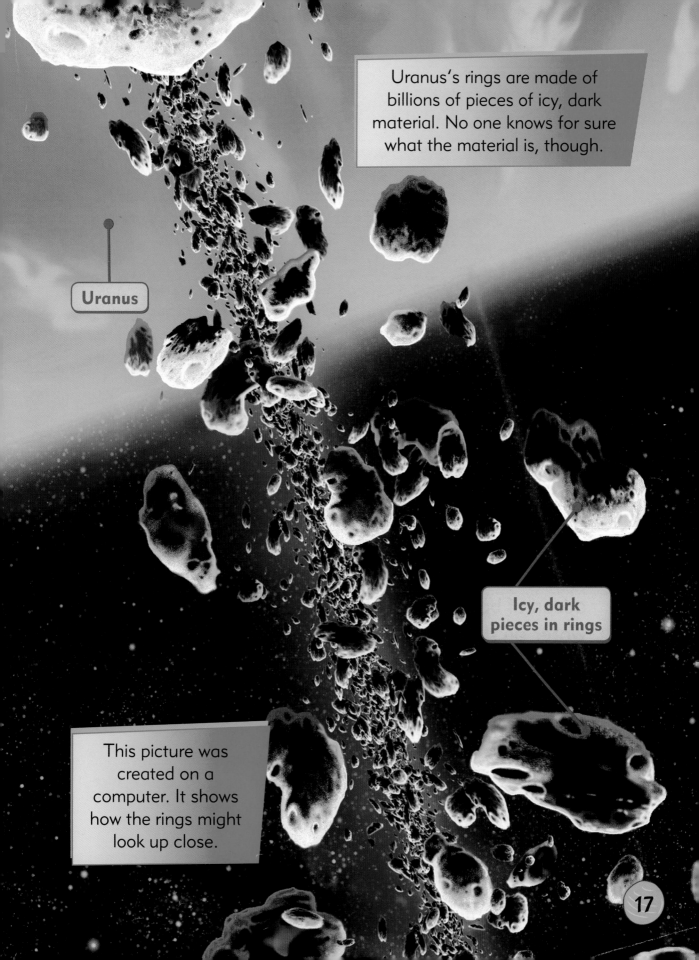

Uranus's rings are made of billions of pieces of icy, dark material. No one knows for sure what the material is, though.

Uranus

Icy, dark pieces in rings

This picture was created on a computer. It shows how the rings might look up close.

A Mission to Uranus

In August 1977, the space probe *Voyager 2* blasted off from Earth.

In January 1986, it reached Uranus and did a close **flyby**.

Voyager 2's meeting with Uranus lasted just five and a half hours.

During that time, the probe found 10 new moons and two new rings circling Uranus.

It also discovered an ocean of boiling water on the planet!

Rocket

Voyager 2 blasts off from Earth aboard a rocket.

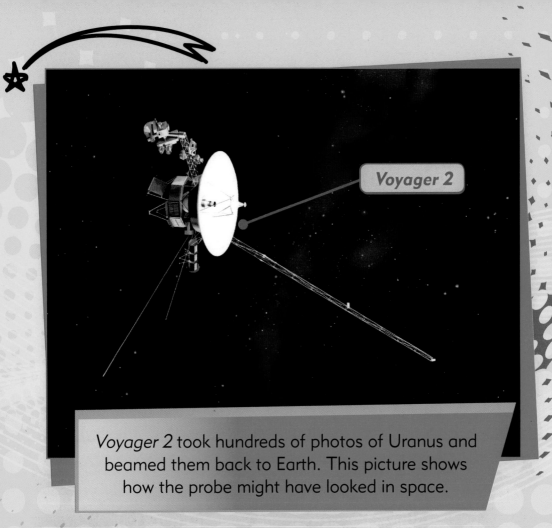

Voyager 2

Voyager 2 took hundreds of photos of Uranus and beamed them back to Earth. This picture shows how the probe might have looked in space.

Voyager 2 took this photo of Uranus.

Uranus Fact File

Here are some key facts about Uranus, the seventh planet from the Sun.

Discovery of Uranus

Uranus was discovered in 1781 by William Herschel. Other people had seen Uranus through telescopes, but Herschel was the first to say for sure that it was a planet.

How Uranus got its name

The planet is named after the Greek god of the sky.

Planet sizes

This picture shows the sizes of the solar system's planets compared to each other.

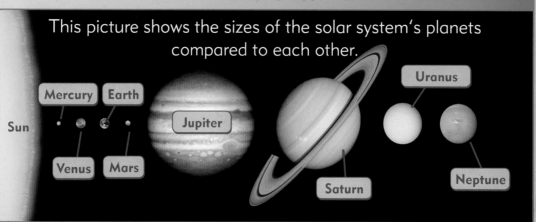

Sun

Mercury Earth

Venus Mars

Jupiter

Saturn

Uranus

Neptune

Uranus's size

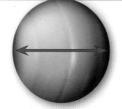

About 31,518 miles (50,724 km) across

How long it takes for Uranus to rotate once

About 17 Earth hours

Uranus's distance from the Sun

The closest Uranus gets to the Sun is 1,699,449,110 miles (2,734,998,229 km).

The farthest Uranus gets from the Sun is 1,868,039,489 miles (3,006,318,143 km).

Length of Uranus's orbit around the Sun

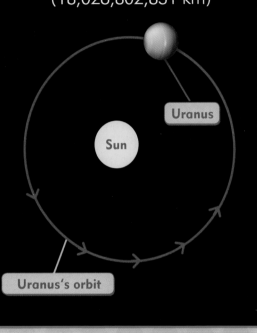

11,201,335,967 miles (18,026,802,831 km)

Uranus

Sun

Uranus's orbit

Average speed at which Uranus orbits the Sun

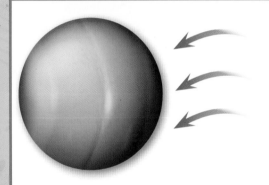

15,209 miles per hour (24,477 km/h)

Length of a year on Uranus

30,687 Earth days (about 84 Earth years)

Uranus's Moons

Uranus has at least 27 known moons. There are possibly more to be discovered.

Temperature on Uranus

-357°F (-216°C)

Get Crafty
Zoom Into Space Game

Travel through the solar system by inventing your own board game.

Divide a large, square piece of construction paper into 25 squares. Draw or paint planets, moons, the Sun, asteroids, and comets on the squares. Now make up the rules of your game, and zoom into space with a friend!

Game Ideas
Here are some ideas to get you started:
- Try throwing a dice and moving that number of squares. What happens when you land on a picture?
- Maybe you get 10 points for landing on the Sun, or 5 points for a planet.
- Perhaps you have to go back 2 squares if you land on an asteroid.

Glossary

asteroid (AS-teh-royd) A large rock that is orbiting the Sun. An asteroid can be as small as a car or bigger than a mountain.

atmosphere (AT-muh-sfeer) A layer of gases around a planet, moon, or star.

canyon (KAN-yun) A deep valley with steep sides.

collision (kuh-LIH-zhuhn) A crash between two objects.

comet (KAH-mit) A space object made of ice, rock, and dust that is orbiting the Sun.

dwarf planet (DWARF PLAN-et) A round object in space that is orbiting the Sun. Dwarf planets are much smaller than the eight main planets.

flyby (FLY-by) A flight by a spacecraft past a planet, moon, or other body in space. A flyby takes the spacecraft near the planet in order to study it closely and send information back to Earth.

gas (GASS) A substance, such as oxygen or helium, that does not have a definite shape or size.

moon (MOON) An object in space that is orbiting a planet. Moons are usually made of rock, or rock and ice. Some are just a few miles wide. Others are hundreds of miles wide.

orbit (OR-bit) To circle, or move around, another object.

planet (PLAN-et) A large object in space that is orbiting the Sun. Some planets, such as Uranus, are made of gases and liquids. Others, such as Earth, are made of rock.

probe (PROBE) A spacecraft that does not have any people aboard. Probes are usually sent to planets or other objects in space to take photographs and collect information. They are controlled by scientists on Earth.

rotate (ROH-tate) To spin around.

solar system (SOH-ler SIS-tem) The Sun and all the objects that orbit it, such as planets, their moons, asteroids, and comets.

Index

Read More

Hughes, Catherine D. *First Big Book of Space (National Geographic Little Kids)*. Washington, D.C.: The National Geographic Society (2012).

Rosa, Greg. *Uranus: The Ice Planet (Our Solar System)*. New York: Gareth Stevens (2011).

Learn More Online

To learn more about Uranus, go to
www.rubytuesdaybooks.com/uranus